Leadership

Exercises In Lateral Thinking And Brain Teasers To Help Students Unlock Their Creativity And Leadership Potential

(Finding The Keys To Success Through The Acquiring Of Management Abilities And Leadership Methods)

Christian Morton

TABLE OF CONTENT

Various Methods Of Leadership 1
Definition Of A Servant Leader 19
Acquiring Social Skills 48
Cultivate An Intellectual Curiosity By Doing Things Like 80
Realizing Objectives Via Efficient Implementation 113
Leadership Theories 130
Conclusion 150

Various Methods Of Leadership

Are you aware of your personal style?

In order to grasp the true essence of servant leadership, it is imperative to have a comprehensive understanding of the various forms of leadership. The leader should engage in self-evaluation to discern their inherent leadership style. This will assist in fostering a more informed assessment in support of team guidance.

Observers can discern when a leader demonstrates insincerity in their self-representation. Exhibit authenticity and maintain a steadfast approach in guiding the team. Engaging in an unnatural manner will create an aura of ambiguity and cast doubt upon your capacity to assume a leadership role.

Every leadership style possesses its own distinctive characteristics, and depending on the specific circumstances at hand, you will deploy one style in preference to another. The bedrock of effective leadership will serve as a compass in determining the most optimal approach to employ. There exists no miraculous amalgamation that guarantees success. Each circumstance is examined to determine the most optimal course of action.

In the year 1930, Lewin established a framework encompassing three distinct leadership styles rooted in the field of psychology: autocratic, democratic, and laissez-faire. These styles continue to be widely employed in contemporary contexts for the purpose of defining different leadership approaches.

The autocratic style necessitates prompt adherence. As the term suggests, this is a leader who adheres strictly to a culture of compliance and obedience. This particular leadership style may be recommended in circumstances necessitating urgent action. Nevertheless, continuous utilization of it will inevitably lead to dissatisfaction within the team. This methodology demonstrates efficacy in safely evacuating individuals from a burning structure or a situation involving gunfire. It demonstrates efficacy when employed during a code or within the critical care unit in instances of cardiac arrest. It is counterproductive to modify the behavior of our team and is often met with resistance. Exercise caution when utilizing it.

The democratic approach entails achieving consensus through active participation. The democratic leader is someone who fosters trust and accomplishes objectives through the means of voting, consensus-building, or collaborative efforts. This type of leader has a propensity for posing inquiries and attaining consensus. Take this approach into account when implementing a new process or initiative. Establish a compact focus group tasked with delineating the process, expectations, workflow, and other pertinent aspects. There will invariably exist elements that escape your consideration due to the lack of daily engagement in the job. Summon your subject matter experts (i.e., team members) and engage in cooperative endeavors. This will additionally serve as a means for obtaining the team's agreement and participation.

The laissez-faire approach is rooted in the ideology of fostering a robust team and refraining from excessive intervention or interference. It represents a contrast to autocratic leadership. In this context, individuals are provided with objectives and goals that possess flexible definitions. An invaluable advantage inherent to this approach is its propensity for fostering innovation. This particular style may prove vexing to individuals seeking unambiguous objectives.

In the year 1964, the individuals of corporate orientation, namely Robert Blake and Jane Mouton, directed their attention towards a bifurcation of styles: one centeredaround tasks, and the other focused on individuals.

A task-centric approach prioritizes the attainment of outcome-oriented results. In this manner, the leader ensures precise communication and establishes explicit expectations regarding the objectives and desired outcomes. The assessment of the most suitable individual for the assignment is not taken into account.

The people-centric approach emphasizes the evaluation of team members' current skill set, level of interest, and personal growth to determine the most suitable individual for a particular task. This approach proves highly effective in fostering personal growth through the provision of challenging opportunities. Stretch opportunities encompass assignments entrusted to individuals, surpassing their existing skill set, aiming to encourage them to venture beyond their comfort zone for personal growth and advancement.

Daniel Goleman effectively outlined the six distinct emotional styles of leadership, namely visionary, coaching, affiliate, democratic, pacesetting, and commanding, in 2002.

The visionary approach inspires individuals to strive towards a clear and compelling vision. It is widely acknowledged that this style of leadership holds significant influence. This type of leader derives strength from their profound commitment and visionary outlook. The coach instills a sense of empowerment within the individuals. This approach underscores the team's capacity for growth and motivates them to achieve their full potential. It frequently serves as a catalyst for innovation and the cultivation of creativity. Articulate the overarching mission and remove any obstacles impeding the progress of the team.

The coaching style facilitates the development of individuals in preparation for their future endeavors. This is a type of individual in a leadership position who prioritizes the attainment of advancement. Each and every member of your team is in need of coaching to varying degrees. The objective of the individual may not align with pursuing a career in management. Directing one's attention to the objective of the individual could be as uncomplicated as exemplifying utmost proficiency in my daily tasks or augmenting my expertise in the management of diabetes.

The affiliate style fosters emotional connections. This leader prioritizes the welfare of individuals by making sincere efforts to establish interpersonal connections. It demonstrates optimal efficacy during the motivational phase, particularly in instances where a deficit of motivation exists within the team. It is crucial to employ this style when engaging in conversations with higher-ranking executives. You serve as the representative of the team, having been selected by the team members. Please bear this in mind and exercise due diligence when considering the potential effects of new initiatives on the team.

The pacesetter approach demands utmost excellence and self-guidance. This is the type of leader who exhibits a tendency to establish elevated standards without due regard for input from others. When employed, it can undermine their morale and impart a sense of inferiority.

The utilization of pacesetting is suitable when defining and implementing a benchmark for the provision of care. A case in point would be our approach of classifying our patients with diabetes as effectively managing their condition when the A1C level is at or below 7 percent. Utilizing pacesetting as a means to enhance productivity yields inefficacious results. Our objective as clinical professionals is to enhance the management of diseases for our patients. Enhancing disease management mitigates the potential for complications. Complications associated with diabetes encompass vision loss, renal replacement therapy, and surgical removal of extremities. Maintaining such a stringent criterion is of utmost importance for this particular team.

I have previously conveyed my gratitude for the opportunity to assume the leadership of a prominent biotechnology enterprise. The initial round of Town Hall meetings that I conducted provided me with a comprehensive understanding of the formidable challenge that lay ahead in order for me to establish a presence in the resilient local community I had been advised about. I encountered multiple obstacles that I had to surmount. Specifically, I was not a local resident hailing from the Southern region, and I lacked firsthand exposure to the Biologics Drug Substance manufacturing industry. I was brought on board with the responsibility of spearheading a comprehensive overhaul of the organization's performance across various aspects, including financial, quality, and safety. The potential for growth and success in this business was substantial; nevertheless, there was a lack of cohesive collaboration and interdependence among its employees across different departments and teams. The organization's silos presented a problem. Indeed, while it is evident that the individuals possessed commendable proficiency and extensive expertise, it is worth noting that the collective performance of each group had significant repercussions on the work undertaken by other groups. The lack of clarity in the transition of output from one area to another hindered the overall operational rhythm essential for large-scale manufacturing facilities. The organizational misalignment has gradually developed over time due to the rapid growth of the company. Consequently, much of the organization's historical cohesion has been eroded, primarily as a result of management's lack of tangible focus on cultivating a sense of intimacy. Based on my assessment, it appeared that the organization had forfeited its essence and clarity of mission; and, to some extent, observing the inner dynamics of the organization felt akin to witnessing individuals mechanically complete each day's tasks.

After conducting an initial Town Hall in which I introduced myself as the new leader, shared pertinent information about my background, and elucidated my expectations for the organization as well as what the organization can anticipate from me, I dedicated substantial resources to the organization. I encountered individuals in the cafeteria, at their respective workstations, and most notably within the operations and utility/maintenance centers. I dedicated a portion of my time to working in operations during the late evening shifts and throughout the weekends. I was endeavoring to identify two pivotal components of the prevailing culture:

Who are the individuals holding leadership positions within the organization that may not be clearly identified in the organizational charts? Each and every organization comprises individuals with undisclosed roles as influential figures shaping the corporate culture. Regrettably, management frequently categorizes these individuals as "disruptors" or individuals who cause inconvenience. Indeed, these anonymous influencers play a pivotal role in acquiring the necessary impetus for progress and metamorphosis.

What indications of organizational remnants can be observed, highlighting initiatives that were not further pursued by the organization? In each business enterprise that I have overseen during a period of transformation, the lingering impact of prior investments in external consultancy services can be discerned, reminiscent of antiquated graphs displayed on the walls. Management, whether at the corporate or local level, has often been inclined to invest in fleeting trends or initiatives, creating temporary enthusiasm among certain individuals. However, they frequently fail to follow through or sustain their commitment to these initiatives. In every instance I have investigated (and this holds true in the context of this industry as well), remnants of previous endeavors can be discovered. In summary, I have determined that it is preferable to refrain from initiating change rather than initiating it and allowing it to become lost within the nebulous realm of corporate initiatives. In essence, there exist individuals who wholeheartedly support the initiative and embrace it as advocates, whereas there are inevitably dissenters who respond with skepticism and a sense of repetition. Regrettably, the failure to execute these initiatives or maintain a steadfast commitment to a fresh approach only strengthens the detractors' ability to substantiate their prognostications of skepticism.

Initiating Efficient Communication
Ineffective communication can be detrimental to a team's success as it hinders the collaboration and coordination necessary among its members. Leaders serve as the central hub of this communication process. They actively mitigate any potential communication gaps that may arise both internally within the team and externally with upper management, as these can lead to conflicts or costly mistakes.

They possess the capacity to effectively oversee communication by fostering an atmosphere wherein individuals feel at ease in actively exchanging information. This interaction entails active engagement in both speaking and listening, fostering an optimal equilibrium for effective communication. Leaders are adept at disseminating information and willingly solicit and consider input from their teams.

Managing Time and Productivity

Leaders bear the responsibility for the performance of their teams. This encompasses adhering to deadlines and fulfilling the required deliverables. They are capable of doing so by virtue of possessing the following:

Effective Time Management Abilities – Competent leaders possess exceptional abilities in managing their time, enabling them to effectively steer their teams towards successful project completion. They possess the capability to establish priorities and determine the order in which tasks should be completed, thereby preventing the need to rush or cram in order to meet all obligations. They demonstrate the ability to discern between pressing matters and those of greater significance, and accordingly develop a timetable to provide guidance to their colleagues.

Proficiency in Organization – Exemplifying adeptness in organizational abilities is a hallmark of effective leaders, exhibited through their own assignments as well as their adept management of their teams. They establish lucid objectives comprehensible to all stakeholders, thereby eliminating any ambiguity concerning the required actions. They engage in strategic planning by assigning tasks to individuals who possess the requisite skills for their execution. This to a great extent guarantees optimal efficiency during the completion of the task.

Effective Problems Solving Proficiency – Astute leaders acknowledge that endeavors and assignments often encounter obstacles throughout their course. It is essential for them to be prepared to handle these issues continuously, as they can significantly impact the productivity of their teams. They have the capability to discern the underlying source of the problem and ascertain the optimal solution, thereby minimizing any potential delays.

Definition Of A Servant Leader

When considering the concept of leadership, do we primarily associate it with the figure of the leader or the individual fulfilling the role of the follower? Interesting, isn't it? Although the essence of leadership lies in guiding and overseeing others, leaders themselves inevitably come to mind as we contemplate the concept of leadership. We ought not to hold the leaders accountable for engaging in the same actions, correct? Do the leaders prioritize self-centered leadership or prioritizing the well-being of others? What teachings does the Bible impart on this matter?

In an era where contemporary business practices prioritize the pursuit of personal gain above all else, the Servant Leadership paradigm embodied by Jesus emerges as a striking counterpoint. A significant portion of our current practices within the church are shaped by the influence of the business sector. Goals and objectives serve as metrics for assessing one's efficacy. We uphold the principle of self-actualization as an esteemed virtue and evaluate a leader's success based on the magnitude of their following. In stark juxtaposition to the global approaches to progress, the principles propagated by Christ implore us to embrace humility, shoulder our burdens, and emulate His leadership as a sacrificial means to facilitate the advancement of others.

Robert Greenleaf, widely recognized as the progenitor of contemporary secular literature pertaining to Servant Leadership, articulates this sentiment about assessing one's aptitude as a Servant Leader. The most effective assessment entails determining whether those in service experience personal growth, enhanced health, increased wisdom, greater autonomy, and a higher likelihood of assuming leadership roles themselves. Hence, a true Servant Leader empowers their followers to surpass their own achievements. The apprentice surpasses the mastery of the mentor. The pupil surpasses the instructor in sagacity.

While conducting my doctoral dissertation, I was presented with the task of establishing a comprehensive definition for the concept of a Servant Leader. This is my definition:

A Servant Leader is an individual who dedicates oneself to nurturing the growth and development of another person to such an extent that the latter experiences improvement in various aspects, including but not limited to their knowledge, stature, prosperity, well-being, contentment, affluence, and recognition, surpassing that of the leader.

Are these ideas noble, albeit pragmatic in nature? Does this question possess a heightened relevance for us within the contemporary Church context? Whom do we observe experiencing growth within contemporary churches and Christian organizations? Do we observe the Leaders' elevation in prominence, affluence, intelligence, well-being, and other facets. Alternatively, do we observe the congregation members surpass the leader in their development? To what extent will leaders willingly and altruistically facilitate the growth of their disciples beyond their own personal development?

Let us contemplate this matter, drawing upon two instances from biblical literature.

INTERACTIONS WITH PEERS AND SUPERIORS IN THE WORKPLACE

Regrettably, numerous companies have adopted the ancient maxim 'Divide and conquer' as a guiding principle.

The underlying principle of this motto is that the competition, jealousy, and disharmony that give rise to the well-known "war between the poor" are advantageous to the management of a company, as they make it increasingly challenging for dissenting voices to unite against any decision made by the leadership.

Past records indicate, nevertheless, that the most triumphant firms are those in which interpersonal connections among colleagues are steadfast and cohesive.

It is preferable to cultivate a strong workforce with shared values, even if occasionally divergent from those of management, rather than fostering a contentious environment where colleagues resent one another but strictly adhere to directives from upper management.

This fundamental principle can also be applied in the context of the majority of team sports. When players come together with a shared purpose, they may occasionally differ from the coach's decisions. However, during challenging moments on the field, they will always possess the determination to face adversity head-on and find the resilience to respond.

However, players who adhere to the coach's instructions lacking a solid rapport and genuine cohesion amongst themselves, will find it increasingly difficult to regroup as a united team and overcome challenging situations.

The concept is straightforward: a coach should not prioritize gaining unconditional affection from his players, but rather undertake the arduous responsibility of fostering a cohesive unit, wherein individuals consistently display readiness to selflessly devote themselves to their fellow teammates.

To prevent being an insignificant part of the organization, it is crucial for a company to ensure that the principles and practices of human resource management are effectively disseminated and embraced by all employees throughout all tiers of the company.

It is fruitless for my team to adhere diligently and coherently to my instructions when they consistently receive accolades for individuals from external sectors or divisions who fail to exemplify our organizational values in any manner.

Hence, for me to earn respect as a manager, it is imperative that I engage in ongoing discussions with colleagues who are at an equal or higher level within the organization. This is to ensure that the management approach employed for the staff is collectively shared.

The efficacy of a company is solidified when all levels of its top management, including the highest echelons, express concurrence with this particular human resource management procedure.

Establishing a collective organizational vision and mission could serve as the initial measure in this pursuit.

It is imperative to instill complete trust in the managers assigned to each division. If the effective administration of human resources is solely entrusted to a single or limited number of managers, it becomes arduous to bring about comprehensive transformation within the organization.

Regardless, it is imperative that each business division be treated with distinct management strategies. By conducting yourself in a consistently confident manner and effectively transmitting this atmosphere to your employees, you can significantly enhance success and yield superior outcomes compared to sectors lacking clear objectives and relying on fortuitous staff management.

3. It is important to bear in mind that in situations where you find yourself disagreeing with a suggestion put forth by someone, there is a possibility that their suggestion holds merit.

It is alluring to allow one's personal opinion of someone to influence their assessment of the quality of her ideas.

If one harbors dislike towards someone, it is likely that they possess a preexistinginclination to regard her suggestions as lacking value.

Don\\\'t do it.

Disregard any preconceived notions you may have about individuals. Listen with open ears. You might learn something. You might improve.

It is possible that such a suggestion could potentially pave the way for previously non-existent opportunities.

If you choose to be petty, you will impede your ability to undertake that course of action.

Now Move Ahead

An essential aspect of maturity and leadership involves maintaining self-awareness and a commitment to truthfulness.

Not everyone may be to your liking. It is indeed a veritable fact that irrespective of one's utmost efforts, it is inevitable that one's affections towards individuals may vary. It\\\'s okay. By expressing unwavering commitment to treating others with respect, irrespective of circumstances, you will attain the ability to accomplish tasks effectively.

And you shall embody the leadership qualities that you have aspired to.

And who knows? You have the potential to transform an adversary into an ally.

Build a solid groundwork for your leadership

All triumphant leaders possess fundamental values and principles that serve as the bedrock of their leadership. These attributes distinguish them from unseasoned leaders. Right from the outset, consider the values and principles you intend to infuse into your distinctive style of leadership.

Within this group, it is essential that you establish integrity as the fundamental bedrock of your leadership style. If one consistently demonstrates integrity, their followers will perceive them as trustworthy. They will have unwavering confidence in the fact that your suggestions and actions are undertaken with the sole intention of advancing the team.

In addition to adherence to integrity, it is imperative to encompass productivity and diligent effort as integral components of the principles that you embrace. Additionally, you have the option of incorporating a positive mindset and a drive for success. You may also add the perpetual pursuit of personal development to the inventory.

The decision regarding which values you wish to incorporate into your unique brand of leadership lies within your purview.

Converse and conduct yourself in alignment with your selected qualities of leadership.

Once you have selected the values and principles that you wish to establish as the underpinning of your leadership, let them serve as the cornerstone for your decision-making process during your day-to-day leadership responsibilities.

Considering integrity as the cornerstone of your leadership, for instance, will prevent you from engaging in any form of deceit, whether it be through words or actions. You will consistently prioritize ethical and equitable considerations in your decision-making process.

In order to instill a strong work ethic in your team, it is imperative that you exemplify that characteristic as well. Demonstrate your prowess as a competent leader by exhibiting diligent effort. Additionally, establish a routine of being the earliest to arrive at the workplace each workday and ensure your presence with the team when your guidance and support are most required. Leaders who uphold the alignment between their words and actions are perceived as possessing greater credibility and trustworthiness by their subordinates. Research findings indicate that this particular style of leadership has proven to be more efficacious in enhancing employee morale, productivity, and engagement in the workplace.

Conversely, leaders who are perceived as lacking integrity foster an environment characterized by skepticism and doubt within the organization. Consequently, this results in diminished employee morale and subpar performance.

May I inquire if you are inside the enclosed compartment?

Are you deceiving yourself? This question poses a challenge in terms of providing a straightforward response. Indeed, one might even harbor the assurance that self-deception is an utter impossibility. In order to emerge from confinement, it is imperative to first acknowledge one's state of confinement.

Take into account the subsequent inquiries:

Are you satisfied with your current employment situation?

Are you genuinely occupied or are you attempting to conceal any shortcomings in your time management abilities?

Are you genuinely inclined or obliged to engage in extended working hours, or are you employing it as a pretext to evade non-work related matters?

Are you genuinely making these decisions due to a lack of alternative options, or are you engaging in self-deception to evade accountability?

Please respond to these questions to the best of your ability with utmost honesty. Please thoroughly consider your responses. Once you are capable of honestly responding to these inquiries and have recognized your current confinement, you will be prepared to initiate the process of extricating yourself from the confines.

Stepping Beyond Conventional Boundaries:

In order to improve your leadership abilities, it is imperative that you think innovatively and move away from conventional methods. Regrettably, we do not have a comprehensive guide outlining the sequential steps to disengage oneself from the confinement of the box. To successfully extricate oneself from the confinements of the box, it is imperative to possess a genuine desire to transcend its limitations. If one intends to ascertain a particular conduct in order to extricate oneself from the confines of a certain situation, one shall not succeed in doing so. All conduct achievable within the confines of the defined parameters may also be achieved beyond the established boundaries. To facilitate one's departure from a limited mindset, it is imperative to shift our perception of individuals, refraining from objectifying them, and ceasing to engage in antagonistic interactions with others. When one relinquishes resistance towards others, they transcend their limitations.

The individuals comprising your team possess needs, aspirations, desires, and apprehensions of equal significance to them as your own are to you. It is imperative for you to acknowledge and accept this as an undeniable truth. The individuals comprising your team should not be regarded as mere pawns to be manipulated according to your own preferences.

In conclusion" or "In summary

Engaging in self-deception will significantly impede the development of your leadership abilities. In order to effectively fulfill the role of a leader, it is imperative to recognize individuals within your team as valuable members rather than viewing them solely as obstacles to resolve. When your team appears to be experiencing stagnation, and you are assigning fault to your team, conversely, they are placing the blame on you. Rather than assigning blame, direct your attention towards identifying a resolution to the issue at hand, which will ultimately contribute to the enhancement of your entire team. Once you achieve the ability to perceive individuals on your team as individuals rather than mere pawns, you will be prepared to transcend your current limitations and embark upon the subsequent phase of your journey. In doing so, you will delve into the qualities that define an effective leader.

Please Contemplate the Following Inquiries:

Do you tend to promptly assign blame to others when your team confronts a challenge?

Could you please confirm that you are currently situated within the designated container?

Would you be interested in stepping outside the confines of the current situation?

Are you prepared to invest the necessary commitment and dedication to enhance your leadership abilities?

Are you prepared to perceive the individuals under your leadership as human beings? Do you possess the willingness to view those whom you are leading as individuals with inherent humanity?

Definition of Loyalty Exercise

In your Journal of Influence and Persuasion, kindly inscribe your personal interpretation of loyalty from the perspectives of a proficient employee and a capable leader, or from whichever kind of superior you aspire to become.

Reflection Questions

Presented below are several introspective inquiries designed to facilitate deeper contemplation on the subject of loyalty. Please record your answers in your Influence and Persuasion Journal as well.

Previously, what were the factors that instilled in you the belief that individuals exhibited loyalty towards you? Did their words, actions, or any other factor contribute to this outcome? Upon deeper reflection of the relationship, have your initial assessments proven to be accurate? Did those individuals whom you believed to be loyal eventually betray your trust, or alternatively, did you yourself betray their trust? Frequently, we express the notion of being a adept or deficient evaluator of character, and by this statement, we are addressing your proficiency in gauging individuals' degrees of allegiance.

What specific conduct or deeds lead you to conclude that an individual is demonstrating loyalty? Which conducts indicate that an individual may lack loyalty or trustworthiness? Do you hold the opinion that your beliefs are equitable? Do your criteria for assessing an individual's loyalty or disloyalty adhere to principles of impartiality and equity?

What is your perspective on the elucidation provided in relation to my characterizations of loyalty? Do you believe my opinion is correct? Do you hold a differing viewpoint from me in specific domains? Do you believe you are capable of maintaining loyalty even as you rest in the passenger seat of your friend's vehicle?

It is permissible to hold differing opinions in regard to my viewpoint, as the concept of loyalty may vary among individuals. Your objective should be to establish alliances with individuals who share a similar understanding of loyalty, as it is significantly more feasible to achieve this than attempting to persuade someone to adopt your own perspective on the matter.

Visionary style
The visionary approach inspires individuals to align themselves with a vision. This is widely regarded as the most influential form of leadership. This

type of leader derives strength from their fervor and clarity of vision. The coach enables the individuals to exert their full potential. This approach instills a sense of confidence and motivation within the team. Frequently, it catalyzes the emergence of novel ideas and artistic expression. Articulate the overarching mission and refrain from impeding the team's progress.

Coaching Style

The coaching approach fosters the growth and preparation of individuals for subsequent endeavors. This is a type of leader whose primary emphasis lies in the attainment of advancement. Every individual comprising your squad requires training in a specific skill. The objective of the individual may not be centeredaround pursuing a career in management. Directing attention towards the individual's objective can be as straightforward as exemplifying excellence in my daily occupation or augmenting my understanding of diabetes management.

Affiliate Style

The affiliate approach fosters emotional connections. This leader demonstrates a genuine commitment to prioritizing the needs of the people, making sincere efforts to establish strong interpersonal connections or affiliations. It proves to be highly efficacious during the motivation phase, especially in circumstances where a deficiency of motivation is observed within the team. It is crucial to employ this approach when engaging in conversations with higher-ranking executives. You serve as the representative of the team, as you have been selected by the team. Please bear this in consideration and exercise caution when assessing the potential consequences of introducing new initiatives to the team.

Pacesetter Style

The Pacesetter style places high expectations on individuals, requiring both excellence and self-direction. This type of leader exhibits a tendency to establish stringent benchmarks without duly considering the input and perspectives of others. When employed, it has the potential to adversely impact their morale and evoke a sense of inferiority. Pacesetting is suitable when setting a benchmark for the level of care. For instance, we regard our patients with diabetes as effectively managing the condition when the A1C level is below or equal to 7 percent. Utilizing pacesetting as a means to enhance productivity is ineffective. As clinical professionals, our objective is to enhance disease management for our patients. Enhancing disease management mitigates the likelihood of developing complications. Diabetes can lead to severe outcomes such as loss of vision, the need for dialysis treatment, and surgical removal of limbs. Maintaining such a stringent criterion is imperative for this particular team.

The topic of democratic style has been previously examined, and once again emphasizes the importance of consensus achieved through active participation. The commanding style can be deemed synonymous with the autocratic style of leadership, as expounded upon earlier.

Transactional Leadership

Transactional leadership places its primary emphasis on the daily functioning of operations. This individual faces difficulties in perceiving the broader perspective or effectively articulating a strategic vision. Transactional leaders place a significant emphasis on an individual's assigned duties and obligations. They institute rigorous performance management protocols for team members falling short of expectations, resulting in diminished morale.

Charismatic Leadership

Charismatic leadership entails the elements of transformational leadership through the means of inspiring and motivating individuals. Nevertheless, it serves to advantage the leader. This leader does not prioritize innovation or driving organizational excellence. This particular approach frequently results in the downfall of numerous establishments.

Servant Leadership

The concept of servant leadership was initially coined by Robert Greenleaf in 1970. It involves demonstrating a genuine inclination to lead by providing service to others, fulfilling the needs of team members, enabling them to make autonomous decisions, ensuring their fundamental needs are met, and prioritizing their personal and professional growth. Frequently, the servant-leader goes unnoticed in terms of official acknowledgment. The servant leader is often deprived of formal recognition on multiple occasions. The leader often remains enigmatic, deliberately directing attention towards the individual colleagues in order to demonstrate their accomplishments. The advantages of adopting a servant leadership approach encompass enhanced levels of engagement among team members, consequently resulting in the attainment of higher performance levels. The colleagues experience a sense of high regard and demonstrate an increased level of dedication. They have a perception that the leaders are cognizant of their well-being and economic advancement.

The team exhibits strong morale by adhering to a moral framework within their guidance. This leader consistently demonstrates exemplary integrity, placing equal emphasis on the well-being and success of the organization and its employees. They prioritize the interests of the stakeholders and possess a remarkable level of self-awareness. The foundational competencies of servant leadership extend beyond all styles of leadership.

Acquiring Social Skills

Embarking on the journey to master social skills can prove to be a challenging and even intimidating task. It is unnecessary to immediately dive headfirst or undertake any significant tasks prematurely. Gradually cultivate your charisma by experimenting with the following strategies and tactics:

Employ music as a means of enhancing your spirits. In instances when one experiences pre-event anxiety, it is advisable to opt for classical, jazz, or even calming classic rock music to alleviate distress and cultivate a composed, optimistic state of mind. If you are experiencing a diminished sense of enthusiasm, I recommend listening to music that elevates your emotions and helps cultivate a more positive mindset. If you are experiencing a sense of self-doubt or low morale, consider utilizing motivational resources to reinforce the belief that you possess the ability to accomplish any goal you commit your mind to. Listen to a beloved DJ mix that will transition you effortlessly from a state of seclusion to becoming the unequivocal life of the party.

Periodically step out of your comfort zone by engaging in novel experiences. Volunteering presents an outstanding opportunity to enhance one's interpersonal aptitude, acquire fresh knowlcdge, and apply acquired knowledge in a non-intimidating context. Additionally, the positive impact it generates within the community intensifies one's sense of gratification. Enroll in a course on a subject of your longstanding interest, and make an effort to engage in conversations with fellow students whenever feasible Attend various gatherings held at your nearby library, offering an additional chance for engaging in social interactions without any feelings of pressure.

Cultivate your capacity for independent action by formulating strategic plans, and adhering to them consistently. Continuing with one's commitments enhances self-confidence as it demonstrates our reliability. Moreover, it bolsters one's self-assurance as the act of persevering eliminates anxiety. We are inclined to develop faith in our ability to carry out the commitments we make, and this significantly enhances our charisma.

Tap into meditation. Engage in structured mindfulness practices, such as guided meditative exercises, where a facilitator verbally leads you through the various stages, dedicating a few minutes each day to foster a state of inner tranquility. Once the practice of meditation becomes acquainted to you, you will discover that attaining a state of tranquility can be achieved effortlessly—particularly beneficial when encountering unforeseen and uncomfortable social circumstances.

Get some exercise. Engaging in a daily 20-minute walk at a moderate pace can effectively contribute to the regulation of one's mental state. Both the body and mind necessitate the presence of these neurochemicals associated with positive emotions for optimal functioning. A continuous surge of endorphins can alleviate a considerable amount of unease and trepidation associated with social situations. Furthermore, you will experience an improvement in your body's overall well-being, resulting in heightened self-confidence that will be manifested through positive body language, thereby effectively elevating your level of charisma.

Set an objective to confront one of your fears. This presents a formidable challenge, yet the potential rewards are substantial. Consider the sense of accomplishment that was experienced during your most recent successful endeavor. Confronting one's fears leads to the realization of possessing the capabilities to surmount challenges and triumph over obstacles. The acquired knowledge from this experience will remain ingrained in both your conscious and subconscious mind indefinitely. Moreover, you will cultivate a sense of empathy for individuals who have either conquered their fears or continue to grapple with them. This task is indeed challenging, but its value will increase tenfold.

Tap into inner creativity. The mind does not find pleasure in idle states. Occasionally, rather than inundating the mind with media, news, and external viewpoints, it becomes necessary to share something with the world that is a reflection of our own originality and perspective. Engaging in the act of creation serves as an exceptional endeavor to amalgamate the various faculties of one's mind into a cohesive and concentrated state. It is not necessary for it to possess the caliber of a gallery-worthy piece or the capability to navigate the Atlantic. Allocate time for self-reflection and engage in artistic pursuits, as they greatly contribute to the development of your self-assurance and nurture your inner sense of wonder. Redesign your environment. Please observe the condition of your living area. Does it possess a somber and disorganized ambiance, serving as a mere retreat where one seeks respite following an arduous day? Allocate a weekend to the task of converting your living space into an environment that fosters inspiration. What are the characteristics of an organized and content individual in terms of maintaining their residential environment? Illuminate the space, maintain cleanliness, and establish a designated area for physical exercise or spiritual reflection. This area serves as a sanctuary for your repose, providing an environment where you restore and rejuvenate yourself upon returning home. Assume the position of being prosperous, and in due time, you shall attain success.

Use visualization every day. Prior to a scheduled engagement, such as a meeting, interview, social event, or date, it is beneficial to engage in the practice of visualizing the desired outcome and envisioning favorable results. In order for professional dancers to effectively develop mastery over new moves, it is imperative that they possess the ability to visualize and comprehend these movements in their mind before attempting to instruct their bodies. Developing the ability to envision favorable outcomes is a pivotal characteristic exhibited by accomplished individuals, as doing so significantly enhances one's likelihood of attaining excellence in their endeavors.

Engage in exercises to cultivate a poised physical demeanor. Even in situations where you find yourself in solitude or without the necessity to present yourself in a certain way, make a conscious effort to engage in the practice regardless. The concept of muscle memory is highly valuable and imperative in the process of altering your nonverbal communication. Maintain constant attention on your posture, and engage in regular exercises for cultivating a poised and self-assured demeanor.

The present moment holds utmost significance. Engaging in the beneficial habit of reflecting on pleasant recollections from the past and envisioning a positive tomorrow is commendable; however, it is imperative to be wary of becoming excessively preoccupied with oscillating between reminiscing and projection, consequently disregarding the present moment. Residing in the present compels us to exhibit our utmost potential in the present moment. Having a keen awareness of the present circumstances can substantially enhance your composure, self-assurance, and charm.

Keep your focus outward. When in the presence of other individuals, direct your attention towards them. This will result in a favorable outcome for you, as their focus subsequently shifts onto you. Introspection exhibited in a social setting can give rise to a sense of unease, along with the potential for any underlying negative sentiments that have been concealed within oneself. Ensure that your mindset remains outwardly oriented, directing your attention towards the world beyond yourself. There are abundant sights to behold, and as you engage, acquire knowledge, and develop, your experiences will be enriched.

Stick with positive people. Acquire the art of selecting your companions wisely. Optimism is infectious, but so is pessimism. By establishing relationships with individuals who exhibit a favorable perspective, you will gradually adopt and cultivate a positive mindset through association.

Administer the content selection for the daily social media feed. Acquire the knowledge of when to abstain from negativity and unfavorable information.

An excessive amount can exert a toll on us akin to contamination or detrimental sentiments. It is of great significance to remain abreast of global events; however, the inherent susceptibility of the human psyche renders one susceptible to anxiety or depression upon excessive exposure to unfavorable news.

Refrain from engaging in the act of comparing oneself to others. You possess a unique identity that distinguishes you from all others. The individual with whom you should solely draw comparisons is your previous self from a year, five years, or even ten years earlier, in terms of personal growth and development. In what ways have you made progress, and in what areas do you require further development? What achievements, significant or modest, have you attained, and how can you direct your efforts towards cultivating a positive sense of self-worth in relation to those accomplishments?

BROKEN CONNECTION

Do you recall our earlier discussion on the three fundamental requirements - namely, affiliation, autonomy, and accomplishment? In these situations, the inherent desire for connection is compromised.

Presented herewith are several indications of a disrupted connection:

When witnessing your child's attempt to interact with a cohort of children, yet facing exclusion from their ranks.

When your child is not included in social gatherings or recreational activities.

When your child is extended invitations for social gatherings, yet conflicts ensue promptly thereafter.

When your child joins, either when friends depart or when the game concludes.

When such situations occur frequently, they have the potential to cause significant emotional distress. One may inquire as to why their child is unable to establish meaningful connections with their peers.

O – One-Upping

One-upmanship occurs when we engage in a comparative analysis of our experiences, attributing increased difficulty to them in response to our child's emotional expressions. Allow me to provide an illustration: "Have you any idea about the considerable distance I had to traverse on foot to reach the educational institution?" This phrase is frequently expressed by numerous guardians. I have observed that I myself have uttered this statement. It seems that you are not fully aware of the challenges I had to endure during my childhood, which were far from effortless. I had significantly more homework compared to you. The tasks I handled were considerably more intricate compared to those you typically encounter. This is so simple. Why are you complaining?

You all reside in opulence. I was solely in possession of a single pencil that was within my permitted usage, and I was never granted access to the assortment of extravagant writing instruments, pencils, and footwear. And still you're complaining?"

Engaging in a constant pursuit of outdoing others diminishes the significance of what resides in the emotional core of our children, hence implying that their individual experiences lack importance.

C – Contradicting

Our child may express, "I do not feel cold."

In light of the situation, our response is as follows: "It is imperative that you maintain a certain level of detachment." The temperature outside is currently sixty degrees. It would be advisable to wear your jacket.

Perchance, they express, "I am not fatigued."

It is currently 8:00 p.m., and it is reasonable to assume that you might be fatigued by now. Considering the extensive duration of your day, which involved both recreation and diligent labor, it is only expected. You must be tired. Go to bed!"

I am deeply disappointed by the actions of my friend.

We refute that by asserting, "Oh, it is not truly unfavorable." Please cease your dramatic behavior and adopt a more serene and composed demeanor. It will be fine."

(I am not suggesting that we should refrain from ensuring that our children wear their jackets and adhere to a specific bedtime routine; rather, I am proposing that their emotional expressions should be acknowledged and validated instead of being suppressed or refuted.) For further insights on facilitating your child's compliance with instructions, including the act of wearing their jacket, please refer to 8.

K – Kiss It

You may observe that when children approach us with minor injuries, we often provide immediate comfort by administering a gesture of affection, such as a gentle kiss, without necessarily investigating the underlying cause. We also apply this approach to our children's emotions; although it is an improvement compared to other methods, it still does not adequately assist them in discovering resolutions for their emotional experiences.

Engaging in the act of 'kissing it' involves providing a superficial solution without sincerely listening to their concerns. We are assuming the responsibility from them and assuming it ourselves. Occasionally, this is justified, yet not consistently. Usually, when employing the phrase "kiss it," our main objective is to promptly resolve the issue, suppress any emotions related to it, and proceed forward. "That sucks. It would be advisable for you to discontinue your association with them," or, "I regret the unfortunate news. Let us explore alternative options to procure a different jacket for your attire." "Allow me to offer you my phone, it shall alleviate your discomfort." "Fret not, for our departure is imminent." "That approach appears to be ineffective. We should refrain from returning to this place in the future.

The combination of your affirmative actions and optimistic mindset leads to the achievement of triumph.
– Shiv Khera

How often have you found yourself observing a woman in her 40s and 50s and being astounded by her youthful appearance and vitality? The key to their physical condition and vitality lies in their optimistic mindset. These women possess a strong inclination towards engaging in social interactions, significantly contributing to personal growth and fostering positive transformations in both their own lives and the surrounding environment. They were adept at avoiding individuals who exhibited toxic behaviors that could undermine their positive energy. They exercised caution in the selection of both their social circle and the surroundings in order to ensure the high quality of their leisure activities.

ArunimaSinha, hailing from Ambedkar Nagar in Uttar Pradesh, is a distinguished mountaineer and renowned athlete. In the year 2011, she was forcefully ejected from a moving train in a brutal manner as she valiantly resisted the attempts of robbers to unlawfully seize her gold chain. She inadvertently descended onto the parallel railway track, resulting in the subsequent locomotive collision that led to severe injury to her left leg below the knee. She mobilized resources from diverse avenues to acquire a prosthetic limb. She exemplifies immense bravery and resilience as she underwent a transformative experience that further fortified her determination to pursue her dreams.

She successfully completed an 18-month mountaineering program and accomplished the challenging ascent of Mount Everest despite the use of her prosthetic leg. In May 2013, she achieved the remarkable distinction of being the inaugural female amputee to successfully ascend Mount Everest, thus etching her name in the annals of mountaineering history Sheharbored no faith in divinity, but rather placed her trust in her own abilities. In the year 2014, her book titled "Born again on the mountain – A narrative of losing everything and rediscovering it" was officially launched by the Prime Minister of India. This literary work delves into the indelible narrative of her unwavering hope, fortitude, and resilience.

In addition, she had successfully ascended the peaks of Mount Elbrus in Europe, Mount Aconcagua in Argentina, Mount Kosciuszko in Australia, Mount Kilimanjaro in Africa, and Carstensz Pyramid in Indonesia. In the year 2019, subsequent to successfully ascending

Mount Vinson in Antarctica, she achieved the objective of unfurling the national flag of India atop the tallest summits across all seven continents.

She was bestowed with the Padma Shri accolade, as well as the illustrious Tenzing Norgay Highest Mountaineering Award, among other notable distinctions. The University of Strathclyde, UK granted her an honorary doctorate. She serves as a source of inspiration for amputees globally. Her perseverance and enthusiasm led to the genuine success that she rightly deserves.

No remarkable accomplishments have ever come to fruition without the presence of sincere ardor.

- Ralph Waldo Emerson

On this inaugural night of Navaratri, I implore you to contemplate upon these attributes that embody the essence of an effervescent woman. Despite the absence of an apparent path, it is imperative to cultivate a mindset characterized by a winning attitude, thereby enabling the innovative construction of a new trajectory in order to fervently pursue one's passion. Immerse yourself in the company of individuals who share similar interests and engage in social interactions with them. This will assist you in persevering, even in moments of doubt caused by setbacks. I kindly request that you cultivate qualities reminiscent of the color orange within yourself. My mother concluded that in order to lead a fulfilling life, it is imperative to embody qualities such as enthusiasm, sociability, and a drive for success.

Interacting with others holds greater value than solitude, which is why gatherings and conferences enjoy widespread popularity.

- MihalyCsikszentmihalyi

I engaged in a deeply stimulating discourse with my mother regarding the distinctive characteristics associated with the color orange. I beseeched my mother to make a return to Bengaluru, recognizing the arduousness that my father and Ajay would face in her absence. And also as Ajay was in twelfth grade, considering his studies, I couldn't afford to be selfish and make mom stay with me at our home town. While everyone else expressed complete satisfaction with the present circumstances, I harbored reservations about this particular resolution.

I exerted considerable effort to persuade my mother to come back, explaining that my conscience was burdened and my peace of mind was unattainable as a result of this course of action. My mother has assured me that she will dispatch a gift to me consecutively for the next eight days, in addition to consenting to engage in nightly conversations with me, commencing at 9 p.m.

The following day, I roused myself from slumber at daybreak in order to assist my maternal grandmother in making the necessary arrangements for the religious ceremony known as pooja. I assisted my mother in assembling her rolling suitcase. She arrived in Bengaluru during the afternoon.

After concluding the evening pooja at our residence, my grandmother and I proceeded to pay visits to some nearby households. Subsequently, in the company of my grandfather, we expeditiously entered the vehicle to embark on our journey to the temple. We were in a rush as we were behind schedule for the aarti. During this nine-day period of Navaratri, my grandmother unfailingly attends the 7 p.m. aarti at the temple. We proceeded towards the Durga temple.

THE TURNING POINT

In the year 2001, our family encountered an exceedingly challenging predicament. The stress started to manifest itself on my internal seismograph, indicating that an imminent catastrophe was on the horizon. Ultimately, on a Sunday afternoon in February 2002, the eruption transpired.

On that particular day, I was fulfilling my responsibilities, maintaining vigilance while my engine was promptly dispatched to an emergency in the immediate vicinity of the fire station. Upon our arrival, concurrent with the arrival of the ambulance, we discovered an incapacitated adult male located on the floor of his modest mobile residence, exhibiting unconsciousness and displaying signs of severely impaired respiration. Currently, our department was still dependent on the assistance of volunteer firefighters, however, none of them were arriving to aid us. The aforementioned circumstances resulted in a heightened sense of frustration on my behalf, thereby exacerbating the present situation. I inquired with the dispatch department to issue an additional notification to the volunteers, and subsequently, I requisitioned the dispatch of a second unit from the fire department to provide assistance. The paramedic encountered challenges when attempting to intubate the patient's airway. I seized the unconscious patient's belt from either side of his body. Exerting considerable effort due to his physical stature, I elevated him from the ground to align his respiratory passage, thus allowing for the insertion of the tube. The patient exhibited evident signs of discomfort, and our team of four was extensively taxed in their efforts to sustain his life.

Throughout the duration, my levels of frustration continued to increase.

Prior to the arrival of the second fire unit, the door swung open and an esteemed member of our team, one of our volunteer fire chiefs, entered the premises. Rather than providing him with instructions on how he could assist, I imprudently expressed my frustration by exclaiming, "Yet another exemplary display of volunteerism!" Amidst the crowded environment, consisting of two paramedics, five members from the fire department, and a sheriff's deputy, we encountered difficulties in maneuvering to place the patient onto the stretcher, extract him from the compact trailer, and transfer him into the ambulance destined for the hospital. The medical professionals requested that one of our party assume the responsibility of operating the ambulance, as well as requiring the assistance of another individual in providing care for the patient. Consumed by fury and driven by an unwavering determination to leave an indelible mark, I proceeded to embark on an exceedingly ill-advised course of action.

The second unit deployed to the emergency scene was the singular ladder truck operated exclusively by the fire department. If I had chosen for both myself and my driver to proceed to the hospital, we could have conveniently left our vehicle parked adjacent to the trailer house, and subsequently arranged for transportation to return. That action would have resulted in the temporary removal of one unit from service. Conversely, I made the decision to operate the ambulance while commanding the officer stationed on the ladder truck to lend aid to the paramedics within the rear compartment of the vehicle. Now, as a result of my decision, two pieces of fire apparatus were rendered out of service, including the sole ladder truck available to us. The decision I made had a significant influence on the caliber of service rendered by Loveland Fire Rescue to the community.

Luckily, no other emergencies occurred during that period. Upon our arrival from the medical facility, we proceeded to Fire Station 1, where I expressed my displeasure and discontent regarding the preceding emergency to my battalion chief, in the presence of numerous fellow firefighters. This specific occurrence took place during a period in our organization's history characterized by a notable level of discord between the paid and volunteer staff members. In light of the strain caused by the organizational conflicts and the urgency to save the life of a critically ill individual, combined with the difficulties my family was facing, and driven by my enduring frustration, I vehemently expressed my anger through a series of emotionally charged outbursts and made imprudent choices.

We are subject to the resultant outcomes that are tied to our actions. I was cognizant of the fact that I had allowed my emotions to exert dominance over my actions. I realized my mistake in succumbing to anger in the manner I did. I was aware of my error in suspending the operation of two rigs. I acknowledge that my behavior was inappropriate and disrespectful when I expressed my frustration and anger towards my battalion chief in the presence of others. However, in a somewhat irrational and self-deceptive manner, I harbored the expectation that it would simply dissipate and fade into oblivion.

Subsequently, I received summons to attend a meeting, which included the participation of our fire chief Mark Miller, the division chief, and my battalion chief, after a span of two days. That particular day will forever be ingrained in my memory as a significant and transformative occasion. Slightly more than four years had elapsed since I was informed by a former shift commander that he was acquainted with my identity and intentions. However, instead of hastily asserting myself in a feeble defense, as I regretfully did in January 1998, I resigned to a state of vulnerability, anticipating the imminent unfolding of my fate.

I was informed by the fire chief that the volunteer firefighter, with whom I had engaged in a confrontation on the preceding Sunday, had initiated a complaint regarding my behavior. In an attempt lacking strength, I conveyed to the fire chief my intention to contact the volunteer and offer an apology, in an endeavor to redirect the scrutiny of the court. The superintendent expressed, "I am confident that you will, Rick." You always do. The issue lies in the repeated occurrence of rock-throwing actions directed towards the glass, necessitating replacement efforts on our part, only for the cycle to persist with subsequent occurrences of rock-throwing. It resembles the window situated behind you, wherein lies an extensive accumulation of rocks that necessitates immediate attention." I apprehended that the higher authority was inclined towards terminating my employment or downgrading my position. I commenced shedding tears, and it was not a deceptive or contrived attempt to elicit his mercy. I was an emotionally fractured individual who could no longer justify or rationalize the presence of my anger.

Cultivate An Intellectual Curiosity By Doing Things Like

Outlined below are three justifications that elucidate the significance of intellectual curiosity:
• It enhances your ability to perceive and contemplate novel concepts. • It cultivates a keenness for exploring new ideas. • It develops your discernment for novel notions. When one experiences curiosity, their mental faculties become actively involved with the particular matter. It endeavors to envision and be receptive to novel concepts that are intertwined with it. When novel concepts emerge, your intellect shall duly acknowledge their presence. If one lacks intellectual curiosity, they may fail to perceive or acknowledge new ideas that come their way. This occurrence arises due to a lack of mental readiness or concentration needed to apprehend them. Similar to attempting to flag down a taxi in London, one will make no

progress if they fail to remain vigilant, and by the time they become aware, the opportunity will have already passed.

- The pursuit of knowledge and inquisitiveness allows one to discover unexplored realms and potentialities, which would remain invisible in its absence. The inability of uncurious individuals to perceive what intellectual curiosity allows one to observe is evident in mundane circumstances and routine endeavors.
- It invigorates your daily experiences.
- It adds a sense of exhilaration to your existence.
- It infuses your life with enthusiasm and zest.
- It generates a feeling of thrill and stimulation in your day-to-day activities.
- It injects a dose of excitement and energy into your way of living.
- It delivers a heightened level of engagement and entertainment to your life. Inquisitive individuals lead captivating lives, brimming with novel knowledge, cutting-edge concepts, and a myriad of captivating subjects that draw their attention. To an individual endowed with intellectual curiosity,

every situation can be perceived as an exciting and stimulating expedition.

Outlined below are several strategies for cultivating intellectual curiosity.

• Keep an open mind. To foster an inquisitive mindset, it is crucial to maintain an open receptivity to discovering novel information, acquiring knowledge, relinquishing outdated beliefs, and embracing the process of continual learning and adaptation. The primary attributes of a receptive mindset encompass a willingness to alter one's opinions, embrace fresh knowledge, and adopt different viewpoints.

• Do not underestimate the value of things. • Avoid assuming that things will always be available or remain the same. A natural inclination for seeking knowledge and a receptiveness to new ideas commonly propel individuals towards the pursuit of research. In order to cultivate intellectual curiosity, it is imperative to consistently scrutinize and interrogate ideas while actively engaging with diverse perspectives. Do not underestimate or overlook things, under any circumstances. Consistently strive to delve beyond the superficial and uncover the underlying intricacies inherent in the surrounding phenomena.

•Ask questions, relentlessly. Engage in thorough exploration to gain further insights into your surroundings. It is widely acknowledged that the questions of what, why, when, who, where, and how serve as invaluable companions to individuals driven by curiosity.

• Refrain from classifying something as tedious. • Avoid categorizing something as mundane. • Abstain from characterizing something as uninteresting. • Desist from designating something as dull. If premature labeling occurs, it restricts the potential for various outcomes. Inquisitive individuals never deem things monotonous, and their intellectual inquisitiveness perpetually unveils fresh opportunities leading to captivating realms. That does not imply that prompt measures will be taken to pursue that new course. The door remains open for the purpose of being visited at a later time. Should immediate investigation not be feasible, rest assured that the human mind possesses the capacity to retain such information, such that when encountering related knowledge in the future, one's inherent curiosity shall rekindle and prompt contemplation anew.

•Engage with a wide range of literary works. To cultivate your intellectual inquisitiveness, I suggest opting for an alternative book rather than fixating solely on a single genre of literature. Engage in the exploration of a work of fiction, or delve into a comprehensive examination of societal events depicted in a historical book, or acquaint yourself with the life story of an individual through a biographical text, or appreciate the beauty and depth presented in an art book, or immerse yourself in the knowledge and discoveries offered by a scientific publication. Choose a new author. And keep going.

- Contemplate the pursuit of knowledge for its intrinsic value.
- Deliberate on the acquisition of knowledge purely for its inherent worth.
- Reflect upon the act of learning solely out of intellectual curiosity. Have you ever acquired knowledge or skills in the absence of any external obligations? Intellectual curiosity is characterized by a perpetual pursuit of knowledge, driven by a genuine desire to deepen one's understanding of a specific subject matter or explore entirely unfamiliar territory.

- Embrace the unknown. Individuals lacking an inclination towards intellectual inquisitiveness often exhibit apprehension towards novel concepts, fear the prospects of alteration, and exhibit steadfast commitment to the prevailing state of affairs. In order to cultivate a fervent pursuit of knowledge, it is imperative to embrace novel experiences, accept and adapt to transformations, and exhibit a resolute courage to instigate transformative actions. Posing inquiries such as 'For what reason?' and 'Why would that not be?' carries profound potency in fostering self-reflection and stimulating one's thirst for knowledge. Engage in this exercise for each individual thought and observe the deductions you arrive at.

Give precedence to the development of human resources.
A coach can assist leaders in enhancing and augmenting their consideration, empathy, and regard for the individuals who collaborate and serve under their supervision.
Collectively, we uncover the potential of acknowledging, motivating, empathizing, and valuing every individual with whom the leader interacts. Can we aspire to cultivate that respect into a profoundly dedicated, consciously intentional manner of existence? One of the gratifying aspects of coaching is the opportunity to facilitate the transformation of my client's aspirations (desired conduct) into reliable and accountable undertakings.

Assume responsibility for one's actions and the resulting consequences.

When offering guidance to a leader who consistently deflects responsibility and avoids accountability in the face of challenges, I will endeavor to facilitate their recognition that such conduct is detrimental and incapable of being maintained in the long term. While it may exhibit human qualities and familiarity, such behavior will erode and undermine their aspirations of wielding influence and earning reverence as a leader.

When my esteemed client comprehends the advantageous ramifications of assuming accountability for their actions and results, it frequently paves the way for a transformative journey of exhilarating self-improvement. Similar to the majority of effective coaching experiences, clients will be prompted to release their attachment to their previous static sense of self, acknowledge, and eventually embrace the malleability of their habits. The leader's egotistical selfdefensemechanism relinquishes its fear-driven influence over the leader's existence and previous manner of conduct.

Provide comprehensive and well-considered resolutions.

Several of the leaders I am responsible for coaching exhibit inadequate communication skills. They convey expedited, curt, and frequently ambiguous messages to their constituents. They engage in this behavior with little to no premeditation. Upon highlighting the perplexing or potentially offensive nature of their verbal expressions to those receiving their message, they exhibit defensiveness and assert, "I articulated my intended meaning." It is their responsibility to address the issue if I did not articulate my sentiments in alignment with their expectations.

I beg your pardon, but the issue at hand seems to lie with you. However, I must inform you that this development is indeed favorable. If you are receptive to an alternative approach, it is possible to enhance it.

Effective communication consists of two essential components: firstly, the manner in which information is conveyed, and secondly, the manner in which it is comprehended. Frequently, those two concepts tend to diverge. If a leader's sole focus and accountability lie in the manner in which a message is articulated, there will inevitably persist challenges in communication. However, when the leader also assumes accountability for the reception of the communication, improvements are promptly observed.

In my capacity as a coach, I occasionally assist leaders in formulating the verbiage and demeanor of their communication. We will assess the potential emotional impact of receiving it. In the event that it is deemed suitable, the leader may also engage in a follow-up conversation with the recipients of the message, asking: "How was this perceived?" Are there any inquiries or suggestions you would like to share?

Enhance value whenever feasible.

Certain leaders whom I have provided coaching to have expressed the sentiment that they are disinclined to extend praise and recognition to others in the manner that differs from their own approach. The desire to project an image of formidable individuals who are not easily impressed frequently serves as the underlying cause for this opposition.

Nevertheless, the efficacy of positive reinforcement as a catalyst has been empirically demonstrated. When the individuals under your leadership perceive themselves to be recognized, valued, and validated, their motivation and propensity to enhance their performance are enhanced.

Do you have a desire to enhance your leadership abilities, or is maintaining your current, outdated persona of importance to you? When engaging in the coaching of a leader such as this individual, it is my desire that they possess a receptiveness to the potential benefits that these practices can provide to their performance and overall level of influence. I refrain from categorizing their actions as "incorrect" since they are not inherently so. It proves to be comparatively less efficient than an alternative mode of communication. If I am able to convince them that the new habit corresponds to their personal aspirations, we can commence the practice phase.

Action step
Using the provided instructional manual, kindly elaborate on a particular instance in which you undertook a workload that exceeded your capacity.

Concern #2: Your approach to learning tends to be excessively passive

This challenge is among the most significant issues encountered by individuals. Allow me to present a fact: the acquisition of knowledge is an active undertaking. Allow me to reiterate: the acquisition of knowledge requires an active and engaged approach. It entails an active process that demands significant exertion. The primary cause for your potential remembrance deficits does not stem from having a deficient memory, but rather from the likelihood that you are not acquiring knowledge in an appropriate manner.

Allow me to provide you with a few instances of passive learning activities that you might presently be partaking in:

Engaging in repetitive perusal of the identical excerpt. In the majority of instances, engaging in a subsequent reading of the same literary work does not enhance one's ability to retain the information more effectively, but rather fosters the perception of acquiring knowledge. The substance may begin to sound recognizable, but that does not indicate that one has attained mastery of it.

Underlining sentences. Underlining or highlighting serves as an additional approach to engender a sense of active engagement and acquisition of knowledge. Nevertheless, it has been demonstrated to be quite inefficacious.

Engaging in passive consumption of podcasts/videos. Passively absorbing any form of information proves to be an inefficient approach to the process of learning. Alternative expression in a formal tone: "Superior approaches encompass the act of rephrasing the material using one's own language or endeavoring to discern the principal concepts mentally."

Cramming. Engaging in intensive study sessions before an examination can undeniably enhance the retention of a substantial amount of information within a concise timeframe; however, it is likely that the majority of the acquired knowledge will be forgotten rapidly.

What about you? Do you have a propensity towards passive learning? What specific actions or strategies could be employed to enhance one's ability to become an engaged and proactive learner?

Action step

With reference to the action guide provided, kindly enumerate two to three specific measures that can be adopted to foster a proactive approach to learning.

Problem #3: The lack of a discernible objective underpinning your educational endeavors.

In numerous respects, we acquire abilities that will enable us to advance towards the individual we strive to become. However, frequently, instead of acquiring knowledge aligned with our true desires, we acquire knowledge that we perceive as obligatory or as mandated by others.

Certainly, it may not always be feasible to acquire knowledge in areas that truly captivate your interest; nonetheless, that should not deter your efforts to do so. Numerous individuals who have achieved remarkable success in their respective fields have attained excellence through their unwavering passion for their work. Indeed, I would assert that passion alone possesses a level of efficacy equivalent to, if not surpassing, all the other instructional methods elucidated within the contents of this book. With an unwavering dedication, one can attain mastery in almost any skill, even with potential missteps in their adoption of learning techniques. This is because:

Devote an abundance of time and exert a higher degree of effort towards the acquisition of knowledge on this subject, surpassing the vast majority of individuals.

Enhance information retention and expedite learning by cultivating a profound emotional resonance with the study materials, thereby facilitating

Persevere relentlessly even in the face of obstacles that may arise during your pursuit, driven by your unwavering passion for the subject matter.

Similar to you, I am currently engaged in the pursuit of enhancing my capacity to learn more effectively. Nevertheless, I continue to make numerous mistakes and succumb to the majority of the typical problems outlined in this section. However, notwithstanding the employment of subpar learning methods, I managed to establish myself as a professional writer, despite not possessing a formal writing degree and not being a native speaker of the English language. My acquisition of writing skills was facilitated by heeding Stephen King's guidance, wherein he proclaimed, "To establish oneself as a writer, it is imperative to devote extensive time to both reading and writing."

Likewise, upon careful reflection, I could have acquired Japanese language skills in a more optimal manner; however, owing to my genuine passion for studying Japanese and dedicating an extensive number of hours to its pursuit, I ultimately achieved a high level of proficiency.

In essence, it is imperative to endeavor to acquire knowledge in areas that genuinely pique your interest. This will enhance your educational experience, rendering it both more pleasurable and efficacious.

17

Acquired Knowledge of Business Strategy

As per the notifications received from the educational institution:

APPLICATION FOR CORPORATE USE

In educational institutions, our routine consisted of morning prayers, a diverse curriculum encompassing various subjects, dedicated time for music education, access to a library, and scheduled physical fitness activities. We experienced significant student participation, and each student remained enrolled at the school unless a parental transfer occurred. We held a deep reverence for our school, perceiving it as a revered institution that facilitated our personal growth. If business organizations can effectively apply analogical considerations, it would result in the achievement of increased profitability. The employees must be brought along within the corporate realm, as if traversing a revered journey of personal development and individual advancement.

What can employers do to ensure that employees maintain a steadfast commitment to the corporate interests, remaining devoted and dedicated until circumstances beyond their control necessitate a change?

KEY MANAGEMENT TAKEAWAYS DERIVED FROM ADHERENCE TO THE ORGANIZATIONAL CULTURE:

1) Implement a daily procedural measure wherein employees are required to partake in a brief corporate oath each morning, devoted to visualizing and aligning with the overarching objectives of the organization for a duration of 5 minutes.

2) Encourage employees to maintain objectivity and ensure effective communication through the circulation of comprehensive documentation, thus minimizing the risk of professional misinterpretation.

3) It is recommended for employees to engage in an evening session of music listening, lasting for 10 minutes, before departing from the office, in order to unwind and reenergize themselves for potential emergency assignments.

4) It is advisable to foster and promote a corporate environment wherein employees are encouraged to engage in

the practice of reading magazines, novels, and newspapers for a duration of half an hour following their midday break. This will serve to instill a sense of participation in the ongoing evolution of societal culture, thus facilitating cohesive teamwork within the organization, while simultaneously discouraging the occurrence of negative behaviors such as engaging in office politics or fostering a toxic work atmosphere.

5) Employers should diligently uphold the well-being of their employees by engaging them in a regular regimen of physical exercise or outdoor activities. By implementing this approach, absenteeism would be effectively addressed and employee productivity would be consistently elevated.

Psychological perspective: The school serves as a fundamental catalyst for human enlightenment in terms of career aspiration, societal conformity, spiritual initiation, ecosystem comprehension, and leadership development. In the educational institution, the development of the subconscious mind encompasses all facets of life. The incorporation of organizational psychology into the field of school psychology should be implemented. Through the practice of collective prayer within the organization, we engage in a meditative state, implanting the 'mission and vision' deep into the recesses of our subconscious. The employment of an objective mode of operation, characterized by the use of clearly defined and precisely articulated job descriptions accompanied by standardized operating procedures, serves to minimize any potential confusion pertaining to the execution of tasks. Furthermore, according to findings in the field of neuroscience, it is anticipated that music exhibits advantageous effects on cognitive processes within the brain. Music consumption has been shown to effectively mitigate levels of the stress hormone cortisol, enhance cognitive functioning, aid in the alleviation of pain (both physiological and psychological in nature), improve memory retention, and enhance physical agility. By engaging employees in physical activities, organizations can achieve both physiological and psychological health benefits, resulting in the addition of greater value to the corporate entity by its employees.

CORPORATE INSIGHT: The cognitive capacity of a child exhibits scientific characteristics. He/She is receptive to acquiring knowledge and developing oneself. If corporations endeavor to encourage their employees to apply the principles acquired in their educational pursuits and align them with the corporate objectives (mission and vision), the prospects for growth would be enhanced, and a thriving organizational culture would ensue. In addition, a state of professional accord would be achieved....

Steps to Profitability

As the leader of an organization striving to enhance its competitive edge and effectively compete in all circumstances, it is imperative that you carefully choose a project with an appropriate scope to evaluate the organization's capacity to establish a competitive advantage. Ideally, it is advisable to choose a product or process that can be comprehensively analyzed and evaluated for potential enhancements within a reasonable timeframe, with the aim of promptly recognizing its success. Therefore, it is of utmost importance to establish a precise delineation of the scope and, if possible, engage the team in actively defining it. The following are the six procedural elements leading to profitability:

1. Set the Vision

As the appointed leader, it is imperative that you establish a well-defined and eloquently communicated strategic vision that aligns with the objectives of your organization. This vision must establish clear and quantifiable objectives for the strategic direction of the organization, such as a desired growth rate in revenue, a revised approach to customer engagement, and a targeted percentage of cost reduction. It is imperative that all individuals within the organization possess a comprehensive comprehension and unambiguous agreement regarding this vision. The team responsible for determining the objectives that will facilitate the attainment of a competitive advantage must thoroughly evaluate and subsequently embrace said vision. The leader is responsible for establishing any necessary limitations and parameters that must be upheld, if deemed necessary. Merely attempting to innovate and devise novel approaches does not guarantee a pristine foundation upon which to build. It is possible that the labor costs have escalated, causing a loss in competitiveness. It would be advisable to explore alternative strategies and seek innovative approaches in order to regain a competitive edge.

2. Establish a Supportive Environment

It is imperative to create a setting wherein the members can experience a sense of safety, even in cases where they may fundamentally differ from the management team's viewpoints. It is imperative that they perceive a climate of transparent and truthful dialogue, thus ensuring that team members are aware of their ideas and concepts being attentively heard and objectively assessed, even in cases where implementation is not pursued. Management has the discretion to opt against utilizing what has been communicated. However, if they perceive that their message has been acknowledged, and a determination is made to pursue an alternate course, provided they hold the belief that their input was duly recognized, they will be inclined to endorse both management's decision and the decision of the collective.

Furthermore, it is imperative to establish a mechanism for incentivizing individuals who develop novel concepts, regardless of whether or not the concept ultimately proves worthy of further pursuit. It is essential to provide recognition to all ideas, thereby instilling a sense of value in individuals regarding their contributions. This will encourage the submission of ideas, even those that may not align with the prevailing mindset of the management. The genuine unleashing of the creative potential of organization members can only be achieved when a conducive environment of this nature is cultivated.

It is imperative to provide individuals with adequate preparation regarding potential measures to be taken in the event that their employment is jeopardized by the innovation. During the 1980s, there was a period in which certain American companies were investigating and implementing the "Just in Time" manufacturing principles, similar to the current situation we are experiencing. Certain organizations implemented a policy wherein no layoffs were implemented for the purpose of process improvements. However, they maintained the prerogative to eliminate positions solely in cases of economic necessity. Ensure that you are adequately equipped to address this matter, as failure to do so will impede your success.

3. Examine the Circumstances and Resolutions

Now consider the potential scenarios for generating a distinctive competitive advantage. The organization must operate within the parameters of the identified vision. They may employ a variety of methods and techniques in order to effectively ascertain a sustainable competitive advantage. Please be advised that the aforementioned suggestions are merely a few examples, as there exists a multitude of alternatives within the extensive range of management and problem-solving literature. A few viable approaches could include:

The SWOT analysis framework, which encompass an examination of strengths, weaknesses, opportunities, and threats. - This model evaluates both internal and external variables in order to ascertain potential areas of opportunity for the organization to explore. - The purpose of this model is to examine internal and external factors in order to identify potential opportunities for the organization to pursue. - Through the utilization of this model, an analysis is conducted on both internal and external factors, with the aim of uncovering potential opportunities that the organization can pursue. This particular model is frequently employed within the context of strategic planning to ascertain the strategic initiatives that merit pursuit.

Ideation - This method is employed to elicit and gather ideas that aim to address the areas of enhancement within the defined scope. It facilitates the swift capturing of a substantial array of ideas. Ideas are documented or recorded on a physical medium such as a sheet of paper or a whiteboard. No deliberation occurs until the entirety of the concepts are documented. Subsequently, these concepts are assessed, and the most favorable ones are subjected to further scrutiny.

Cause and Effect Diagrams facilitate the analysis of the underlying factors contributing to the identified issue, enabling the team to ascertain if the cause has been accurately identified and subsequently address the problem at hand.

In addition, various approaches to discern the optimal course of action are available. These encompass a broad range of methodologies and strategies, such as Mind Mapping, Outlining, and various other techniques, all of which can effectively investigate potential avenues and facilitate the selection of the most suitable course of action.

Please be advised that the practical application of these techniques falls outside the purview of this chapter. Consequently, the recommendations provided herein are intended solely for consideration. Seek additional support or clarification by accessing a range of online sources, literature, or consulting esteemed authorities in the respective fields.

4. Create the Implementation Plan

After the team within the organization has made their decision regarding the product/process that will be employed in order to establish an edge over competitors. The formulation of the implementation plan is required. The plan ought to delineate the extent of the proposed project, outlining the existing or fundamental position in relation to the envisioned future state, which will be achieved as a direct outcome of this project.

The plan should encompass the requisite procedural elements and assignments imperative for the execution of the chosen course of action. It is imperative to ascertain and record the milestones in order to effectively demonstrate the timeline of feature/benefit realization, encompassing any necessary phases in the process. In addition to that, it is essential to appropriately identify all necessary resources, associated costs, and the precise timing of their occurrence. Additionally, it is imperative to identify potential risks and to formulate corresponding mitigation plans to address them.

Realizing Objectives Via Efficient Implementation

We have previously addressed the idea of establishing objectives, strategizing, and coordinating. All information has been recorded and remains unalterable. The moment has arrived to implement your strategy.

The attainment of these goals and plans will hold little significance in the absence of proper implementation.

They will perpetually remain unfinished as no measures were undertaken. This analogy entails the act of initiating the growth of a plant but failing to supply it with the essential elements of water, sunlight, and nutrition required for its nourishment.

This aims to assist you in developing foundational execution skills that will enable you to approach any challenge with ease and familiarity. Allow us to commence the process of molding you into an adept leader who possesses the ability to swiftly embark on decisive actions.

Ease your worries and dispel any restrictive notions.

Apprehensions and constraining beliefs could potentially impede your progress. There might arise apprehensions regarding the possibility of "insufficient quality" or "potential failure". Nonetheless, it is within your capability to gradually overcome your anxieties and self-imposed constraints.

Once these challenges have been surmounted, executing the necessary steps will become significantly more manageable. You will possess unwavering confidence in your capacity to successfully accomplish a goal. Furthermore, your perspective will undergo a transformation, reframing failure as a temporary obstacle.

You have already devised a contingency plan to address any potential setbacks. You can accomplish it with minimal or no hesitation. A genuine leader may experience setbacks, yet they always resurface and regain their position.

Do not hesitate to engage in experimentation. Leaders often exhibit a willingness to take risks. They venture into uncertain territories as they are cognizant of the fact that their triumph hinges upon their own actions and decisions.

Engage in fruitful discourse regarding your objectives and strategic initiatives with your team.

Despite having established goals and plans, it is essential to review them in collaboration with your team. Elaborate on the objectives that must be achieved, the anticipated difficulties (along with corresponding strategies to surmount them), and other related matters. Examine and elaborate upon the necessary procedures to be undertaken by every individual within your team, inclusive of the essential resources and instruments required for successful task completion.

Kindly solicit any inquiries they may have. Facilitate their opportunity to articulate their apprehensions and engage in deliberations regarding potential resolutions. The inclusion of new information or the identification of a potential obstacle may necessitate a modification of plans and goals prior to their execution. Mitigating or averting catastrophe is significantly more desirable than taking action and subsequently observing its occurrence.

When a consensus has been reached among all stakeholders, it is imperative to take prompt action. Please refrain from further delaying this matter.

Make your goals clear.

It is imperative to ensure that the expectations you establish are unambiguous and easily comprehensible. What specific information should be conveyed to each individual team member regarding their respective duties and responsibilities? What constitutes success and what constitutes failure?

Make routines.

Establishing regular schedules will be essential in order to facilitate the implementation process more effectively than has been indicated. What are the duties that need to be fulfilled? What is the systematic process?

Demonstrate to your team members the necessary steps to effectively accomplish the task, thereby facilitating its completion with minimal exertion. It will be an equally straightforward matter, comparable to their mere request for a cup of coffee. In the event of unforeseen circumstances, it is imperative to be ready to make adaptations (and communicate them to your team).

Document and assess any advancements.
We previously alluded to the importance of monitoring your progress in the earlier section of this guide. This entails the meticulous documentation and thorough examination of the key metrics pivotal to the attainment of your objectives. When conducting weekly progress reviews, document observations regarding both successful and unsuccessful elements.

It is possible that you have observed a failure to achieve your daily or weekly objectives. What could potentially be the issue? It may be necessary for you to identify patterns and implement alterations accordingly.

There is a likelihood that one of the members in your team is experiencing some challenges. Consequently, it would be advisable to engage in a conversation with them and ascertain the nature of the situation.

Grant your team members the power and decision-making capabilities.

Your team members have the potential to collaborate effectively when enabling and motivating them to do so. Neglecting such actions could lead to their dissatisfaction, reduced productivity, and a compromised mental state that hinder their ability to accomplish your objectives.

We shall revisit this subject at a later point within this guide. Nonetheless, it is of utmost importance to ascertain that every member of your team experiences a strong sense of inclusion within the larger collective endeavor.

Final Thoughts

Efficient implementation is the driving force behind the progression of plans and attainment of objectives. One is unable to proceed effectively if one's fears and constraining convictions hinder progress. Once you have removed the obstacles, there is nothing that can hinder your progress.

Ensure that your team comprehends your strategies, objectives, and anticipations. Establishing structured routines that render their achievements practically effortless. Naturally, recording progress gives rise to further implementation grounded in said objectives and accomplishments.

8 - The Leader Who Relies on Intuition

Innovations emerge from the depths of intuitive thinking. In light of the matter, it is evident that ideas cannot be deemed as innovative if they have already been devised by someone else. An individual possessing intuition demonstrates an inherent inclination to discern the correctness or incorrectness of a matter based on their internal sentiments. In the event of unforeseen circumstances, individuals turn to their intuition as a means of surmounting them.

A leader with strong intuition is a valuable asset within the team, as their ability to navigate uncertain situations can effectively guide and support other team members. These leaders effectively leverage their abilities and draw upon their prior experiences to intuitively assess the viability of an undertaking. Rarely do individuals have the privilege of an ample amount of time to make consequential decisions; hence, it becomes imperative to rely on one's intuition in order to ascertain the optimal choice for one's team.

How to Become One:

Among all the characteristics, the refinement of intuition is arguably the most arduous task. This is because proficiency in all other attributes is essential for the organic development of this particular trait. However, there exist methodologies that can be employed to augment one's intuition and empower individuals to assume the role of a perceptive leader:

Be curious. Whenever an idea arises, it is advisable to allocate sufficient contemplative time to scrutinize and challenge it. Contemplate whether this proposal possesses a beneficial and viable nature, and if it will contribute positively towards your own well-being as well as that of others. If you encounter a novel stimulus, meticulously observe its functioning and speculate on its origins. Devote careful attention to minute particulars and contemplate the potential rationale for their existence.

Practice self reflection. Prior to retiring for the evening, take a moment to contemplate the manner in which you allocated your time and activities throughout the day. Record your reflections within a journal as a means to enhance your concentration and maintain a written account of your thoughts. Take into consideration the physical, emotional, mental, and even spiritual aspects of your experience. Next, reflect upon potential enhancements for your day and devise strategies to ensure that tomorrow is equally, if not more, successful than today.

Read true detective stories. Numerous accomplished investigators depend on a combination of both the evidence and their intuition when unravelinga enigma. Observe and derive inspiration from their thought processes, allowing them to serve as your exemplary models. Take note of their application of deduction, drawing upon the limited clues at their disposal, to make astute inferences. While perusing their journey, enhance your intuitive prowess by formulating conjectures of your own. As you engage in reading their stories more frequently, you will begin to discern a gradual enhancement in your own growth and development.

One can enhance their intuitive abilities by acquiring knowledge in interpreting the nonverbal cues exhibited by individuals. For instance, explore methods for determining the veracity of individuals' statements, discerning between truthfulness and deception. Please be aware that cultural variances may be relevant.

Rewards Program

After appraising the performance of the employees, it is expected that competent managers will extend commendations and instigate motivating measures to inspire the workforce. This can be achieved by implementing an appropriate incentivization strategy and carrying out the process on a yearly cadence. A rewards program serves as an effective incentive for employees. It facilitates employees' progress in their professional trajectory with a profound sense of gratification and contentment, while concurrently aiding the company in augmenting its employee retention ratio. Presented below are several guidelines for establishing a rewards program.

Annual retreat.

Annually, on the onset of a prominent festive hiatus or nearing the conclusion of the corporate fiscal cycle, arrange for a staff retreat. Depending on the financial position of the company, it is possible that the event will take the form of an extravagant celebration, potentially involving the family members of the employees. It is also possible to host the event at an exotic destination. The retreat is intended to provide an enjoyable experience for the employees, incorporating activities such as team-building exercises, a formal costume contest, a child-friendly performance, and a culminating dinner and dance.

Awards.

Commend the contributions of employees with honors. These accolades may pertain to various classifications of achievement, including titles such as "Top Sales Representative," "Exemplary Marketing Expert," "Premier Operations Director," and the like. In order to acknowledge employees who have made progress towards achieving company objectives, awards can also be presented, refraining from categorizing them as the "best". Cash envelopes may be provided alongside specified accolades. Exemplary individuals may be awarded a complimentary travel ticket to a desirable holiday location. Exceptional achievers may be chosen for salary augmentation or promotion.

Regardless of the type of recognition bestowed, acknowledging employees with an appropriate award provides them with a psychological boost, reinforcing the belief that exemplary performance will be duly recognized and contribute to their advancement within the organization.

Training.

While training serves as a means of assessing performance, as previously mentioned, it can also contribute to the implementation of a rewards initiative. The employees who are chosen for this recognition will view the training as a prestigious honor, particularly when it is held at a remote location that seamlessly merges leisure and productivity. Providing employees with the opportunity to undergo training in scenic mountain or coastal locations, or in international offices of the company, represents a commendable means of recognizing and fostering their developmental progression within the organization.

Footnote: Disincentives.

In the role of a manager, it is inevitable that you will encounter employees who, despite being given ample opportunities, persist as underperforming liabilities. Frequently, employees with such characteristics tend to be nearing the end of their professional journey, or employees who possess dispositions that are resistant to learning and personal development. Employees of this nature could potentially be provided with incentives to opt for early retirement, serving as a possible countermeasure. Employees who continue to display negative performance may be subject to termination. An executive is required to foresee the eventual departure of said employees and take proactive measures beforehand to ensure their exit is handled with minimal disturbance.

Leadership Theories

Within this discourse, a comprehensive examination of two distinct theories shall be undertaken. The initial category comprises Universalist theories, which posit that a singular leadership style is applicable to all circumstances. Another approach is to consider contingency theories, which are based on the fundamental premise that various situations demand distinct leadership styles in order to achieve optimal effectiveness. The theories also acknowledge the influence exerted by environmental and individual variance factors on leadership conduct.

Universalist Theories

a) The theory of the Great Man Approach.

The most primitive and rudimentary perspective on leadership asserted that leaders possess innate qualities and that exemplary individuals throughout history, such as Jesus Christ, Winston

Churchill, Alexander the Great, and Joan of Arc, inherited exceptional attributes like visionary thinking, competence, and affable demeanor. The theory posits that the presence of great personalities within specific lineages implies a genetic basis for leadership. It has been stated that individuals with such traits are predetermined to hold influential positions.

This approach has encountered various criticisms, among which is the concern that its adoption may inadvertently validate the practice of favoritism in staff promotions, as it may result in the integration of individuals who have had personal or professional connections with successful leaders in the past. Furthermore, if we were to accept the belief that leadership is an innate quality, organizations would need to exclusively hire individuals who possess natural leadership abilities. However, this approach is impractical and would render management training programs obsolete, as the recruited personnel would already be born leaders who might not require additional training.

b) The Trait Approach, in accordance with scholarly investigations,
This approach bears resemblance to the 'great man' approach in certain aspects. As an illustration, it depends upon the supposition that the charisma and character traits possessed by a leader play a pivotal role in achieving success in leadership endeavors. However, the distinction lies in its failure to place emphasis on the notion that leaders possess these personality traits from birth. Rather, it posits that specific qualities, whether inherent or developed, are indispensable for effective leadership.

One prevalent issue associated with this approach is the inherent challenge in quantifying select characteristics. Take, for instance, the attribute of "intelligence," a characteristic that poses challenges when it comes to quantifying the prowess of an accomplished leader. In addition, it should be noted that while physical attributes such as 'height' and 'appearance' are readily observable, characteristics of a psychological nature, such as 'perseverance', 'initiative', and 'intelligence', are not easily discernible. As a result of the unobservable nature of psychological attributes, their existence can solely be deduced from behavior, thereby making it susceptible to drawing conjectural inferences. Furthermore, positive traits such as decisiveness, intelligence, and strength are commonly regarded as desirable qualities possessed by successful leaders. However, it is important to note that many leaders frequently exhibit negative characteristics, which may not be explicitly acknowledged or enumerated.

Comprehending the Characteristics of Generation Y

One of the primary factors contributing to the challenges faced by Generation X and Baby Boomers in effectively managing their employees, the majority of whom belong to the Y Generation, is the former's inability to comprehend the latter. Baby boomers lack awareness of the characteristics and traits of Generation Y, which renders leading them to be a challenging task for them.

In the subsequent section, we will delve into the topic of Generation Y in order to gain a more comprehensive understanding of this demographic. The objective of this endeavor is to provide you with the necessary knowledge to comprehend the generation Y and establish meaningful connections with them. Furthermore, we will specifically examine the distinctions between the Millennial cohort and both the Generation X and Baby Boomer generations, with the aim of providing insight into the underlying causes of the generation gap.

Delving Further: Gaining Insight into the Millennial Generation

The Generation Y constitutes the largest cohort in the workforce to have emerged since the sizable baby boomer generation. Therefore, it is imperative for managers, particularly those who belong to the baby boomer generation, as we have previously mentioned, to possess a comprehensive comprehension of the millennial cohort. Millennials possess outstanding expertise, especially in the realm of technology, and demonstrate a notable level of education. Considering the fact that a substantial proportion of Millennials have attained a superior level of education, they demonstrate a noteworthy level of competitiveness and possess extensive knowledge in their respective fields of expertise.

They demonstrate exceptional levels of energy and approach their work with great enthusiasm and fervor. Due to their heavy reliance on technology, individuals find it effortless to engage in multitasking as they possess a variety of electronic devices and appliances to employ while accomplishing their tasks.

The cohort known as Generation Y demonstrates a propensity for establishing lofty objectives, leading to their reputation as a highly driven and ambitious generation. They do not accept mediocrity; they relentlessly pursue utmost perfection. Their aspiration lies in achieving utmost excellence in all their endeavors, thus prompting their integration of cutting-edge technological devices and advanced systems, enabling them to accomplish extraordinary outcomes and optimize their productivity.

Individuals belonging to Generation Y possess a penchant for actively pursuing challenging opportunities and revel in the experience of engaging in a competitive work setting. They harbor a disfavor towards elaborate strategies, especially when they are not the architects of said plans, as their desire entails toiling diligently for their achievements. While they actively pursue challenges within their work environment, they have a strong desire for equilibrium between their personal and professional lives and diligently strive to achieve that equilibrium.

Furthermore, the Millennial generation craves opportunities for social interaction. They are averse to isolation and derive pleasure from engaging with individuals. Hence, they host numerous social gatherings in order to enhance their chances of socializing. This phenomenon is further elucidated by their inclination towards collaboration within a group setting.

Due to the abundant vitality possessed by Millennials, there exists a slight impatience within their demeanor, hence their inclination towards the pursuit of instant gratification. They possess a lack of affinity towards the act of waiting for occurrences and exhibit an inability to maintain patience in anticipation of the manifestation of efforts, especially within extended timeframes spanning weeks, months, or even years. They possess an intense yearning for instant outcomes, hence making them susceptible to diversion as they strive towards attaining their objectives. Due to this rationale, on certain occasions, this cohort encounters challenges in realizing their objectives in the long run.

Millennials additionally desire immediate outcomes due to their appreciation for rapid progress in every pursuit or endeavor they embark upon. The preceding generations view their enthusiasm for swift and accelerated progress as their most notable failing.

Furthermore, individuals belonging to the Millennial generation exhibit a high degree of creative aptitude and actively pursue innovation in all facets of their endeavors. Due to the propensity of monotony to elicit boredom and impatience within individuals, they actively seek alternative methods of accomplishing tasks, thus fostering the emergence of innovative ideas and conceptualizations.

Having provided an explication of the fundamental attributes and significant features pertaining to the millennial cohort, we shall proceed to delve into the underlying factors contributing to the intergenerational discord between the aforementioned group and the preceding generations, notably the Baby Boomers.

6

Learning from failure

Bill Gates

Prior to Microsoft, Bill Gates developed a product known as "traf-o-data," wherein he evaluated traffic information. Unfortunately, this particular product encountered technical glitches, resulting in the company's failure to gain momentum.

The lesson
Bill Gates developed a product that failed to gain traction, prompting him to pursue an alternative avenue that ultimately led to the establishment of Microsoft. One should bear in mind that the failure of a single idea should not deter them, as they are likely to possess numerous other ideas within their intellectual repertoire. It is important to note that many individuals cease their efforts prematurely, foregoing the potential for remarkable success.

Stephen King
One of the literary works authored by Stephen King faced more than 30 instances of rejection in its pursuit of publication.
The lesson
The aforementioned novel has proven to be among the highly popular and commercially successful works authored by Stephen King. This novel faced rejection on 30 occasions before ultimately being accepted.

He achieved this by altering his target demographic.

If a concept proves to be ineffective, it may be beneficial to implement an alternative approach or implement incremental refinements to achieve long-term progress.

Do you recall the individual who opted to resign? No, neither does anyone else.

Steve Jobs

Steve Jobs founded Apple Inc., but following an unsuccessful product launch, he was subsequently terminated from his own company. Following his departure from Apple, Mr. Jobs proceeded to establish another company, which initially faced significant challenges until it was ultimately acquired by Apple. Subsequently rehired by the company, Mr. Jobs played a pivotal role in transforming Apple into the successful corporation it is today.

The lesson

Persevere unwaveringly despite the apparent difficulty of the situation. Steve

Jobs encountered repeated setbacks before ultimately achieving success. Take a moment to consider Apple, a globally renowned corporation that consistently generates a substantial annual revenue in the billions.

Walt Disney

It is worth reflecting upon the fact that Walt Disney was rejected by a company due to perceived deficiencies in his creative abilities. A few of his earlier cinematic endeavors were unsuccessful during that period. These films are presently regarded as exemplary works of art.

The lesson

An initial failure can surprisingly transform into a remarkable concept; it is an undeniable fact that every individual is familiar with Disney, and Walt Disney is currently revered as an exceptionally imaginative mastermind. Consider the hypothetical scenario in which the company that declined Walt Disney's proposal were present in the present day; it is plausible that they would deeply regret their decision.

What I am endeavoring to convey is the importance of persevering, even when faced with daunting challenges. It is often disheartening to witness individuals throwing in the towel when they are on the verge of attaining great success. An unsuccessful endeavor may require slight modifications to achieve success. Irrespective of the number of discouragements you encounter, persevere and continue your pursuit.
Maintain your vision as a focal point and consistently strive to empower individuals to a higher state than when initially encountered.

What does the concept of leadership mean to me?

In my perspective, effective leadership is fundamentally rooted in developing a profound understanding of one's subordinates. It is imperative to possess an understanding of what drives your employees, as well as the ability to motivate and instill inspiration within them.

Consider the exemplary bosses or teachers from your previous experiences, specifically those who have made a remarkable impression. I am capable of considering two, perhaps three possibilities.

Now contemplate the attributes that rendered these individuals remarkable and indelible in your memory. Frequently, these individuals who stand out tend to do so because they have a genuine concern. They displayed genuine concern for the individuals subordinate to them, demonstrating a sincere regard for the welfare, physical condition, viewpoints, and overall prosperity of their employees.

To emerge as a proficient leader, it is truly within one's reach to emulate and replicate the qualities and practices of an accomplished individual. Take into consideration an individual within your personal circle or someone you imagine, akin to a superhero, and emulate their actions. Compile the attributes of these individuals, transcribe them onto a document, and securely store this document alongside your core values and objectives.

Namely, the state of being adaptable without constantly worrying about finances. Being financially stable, rather than focusing solely on material wealth, implies having sufficient funds to cover one's expenses, provide for one's family, and fulfill essential needs. For certain individuals, possessing several thousand dollars in their bank account would be deemed as adequate, while a million dollars would not be deemed as satisfactory for others. Undoubtedly, many individuals perceive financial matters as a crucial component in defining success within our society. However, in the context of defining success, I am referring to the profound sense of liberation, that ethereal breath of tranquility.

The primary aim for the majority of individuals is to achieve financial prosperity, but once a significant fortune is amassed, what follows thereafter?

Hence, it is the rationale behind the consistent involvement of tycoons and individuals of great wealth in various business ventures or charitable initiatives. Many people misinterpret their pursuit as greed, but for those who are already financially affluent, it is the pursuit itself that brings them joy. Using cash is undeniably the most effective method for maintaining a definitive record of the outcome of a competition. It is necessary for individuals to actively engage in the pursuit of their goals or aspirations. There is an urgent requirement to make significant improvements to ourselves, another individual, or a particular entity. It\\\'s simply free will. There is a likelihood that we might relocate or transition.

Self-actualization also significantly contributes to achieving success. This concept can be accurately described as the notion of "actualizing one's full potential," instilling a sense of value and efficacy in one's actions. This signifies that you are not merely putting in a halfhearted effort without any justification; what you undertake and your identity hold significant importance. If, irrespective of any other accomplishments, one experiences a sense of dissatisfaction and purposelessness, the attainment of complete fulfillment remains elusive.

As we embark upon this endeavor of taking the lead and achieving success, it is essential to bear these various considerations in mind as you navigate through the contents of this book. By comprehending the interplay of these thoughts in relation to your overall success, you will enhance your capacity to grasp the means to fulfill your aspirations and do so in a manner conducive to your accomplishments, rather than succumbing to failure. Continue reading to discover how you can attain these levels of accomplishment by means of the four foundational principles elucidated within the contents of this book.

Conclusion

Being an exceptional leader is not a simple task. It necessitates diligent effort and deriving valuable lessons from one's errors. Prominent figures, individuals in positions of authority, and esteemed individuals who have gained recognition globally have experienced various life events that have shaped their identities at present. All individuals commenced their journey on a modest scale and possessed a relatively limited amount of expertise. Nevertheless, after extensive dedication and the assimilation of knowledge over an extended period, they have acquired the skills necessary to cultivate the attributes of an effective leader.

If one aspires to become an effective leader, it is imperative to exhibit a willingness to modify one's present actions. Develop your leadership abilities by attaining the attributes of an exceptional leader. It is pertinent to comprehend that being an effective leader necessitates the ability to fulfill the role of a proficient follower as well. In order to ensure that your voice is heard, it is essential to effectively articulate your thoughts and cultivate the ability to attentively listen to others. In order to be followed, it is imperative that you embody an exemplary role that is deserving of emulation by those in your vicinity.

It is imperative to bear in mind that leadership entails a focus on the collective rather than the individual, emphasizing the team and individuals with whom one collaborates. The world does not center itself around you. Various factors exert an influence on one another, necessitating discerning decision-making in selecting one's courses of action. Continuously engage in innovative thinking and adopt a broad perspective. Always remember to attentively listen to your fellow colleagues. Occasionally, in order to effectively fulfill leadership responsibilities, it is necessary to actively participate as a member of the team.

I would like to express my appreciation once again for your decision to download this book.

I trust that this book has facilitated your ability to discern the optimal attributes necessary for a successful leader. The aforementioned qualities represent only a small subset, yet they are regarded as the utmost essential attributes of an exceptional leader.

The subsequent course of action entails introspection and self-evaluation to identify the specific leadership attributes that require refinement. To effectively lead others, it is imperative to first exhibit strong leadership qualities towards oneself.

In conclusion, if you found this book to be enjoyable, we kindly request that you graciously share your sentiments and contribute a favorable review on the Amazon platform. Your cooperation would be highly valued.

www.ingramcontent.com/pod-product-compliance
Lightning Source LLC
Chambersburg PA
CBHW052142110526
44591CB00012B/1819